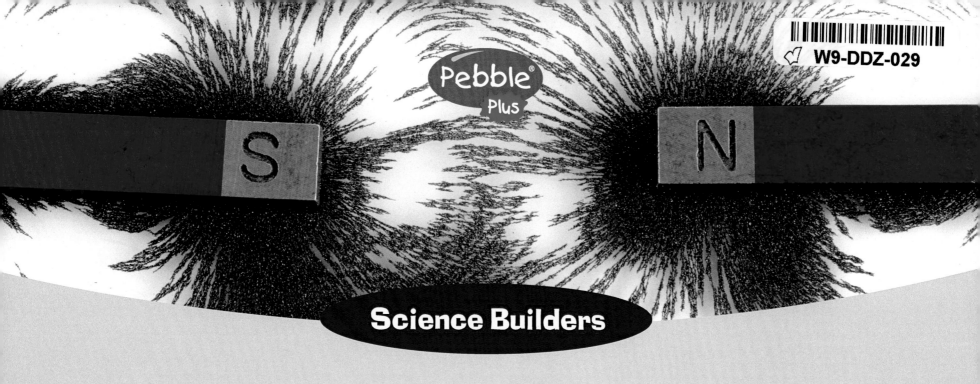

Pebble® Plus

Science Builders

A Look at Magnets

by Barbara Alpert

Consulting Editor: Gail Saunders-Smith, PhD

Consultant: Joanne K. Olson, PhD
Associate Professor, Science Education
Center for Excellence in Science & Mathematics Education
Iowa State University, Ames

CAPSTONE PRESS
a capstone imprint

Pebble Plus is published by Capstone Press,
1710 Roe Crest Drive, North Mankato, Minnesota 56003.
www.capstonepub.com

Library of Congress Cataloging-in-Publication Data
Alpert, Barbara.
  A look at magnets / by Barbara Alpert.
      p. cm.—(Pebble plus. Science builders)
  Summary: "Simple text and full-color photographs provide a brief introduction to magnetism"—Provided by publisher.
  Includes bibliographical references and index.
  ISBN 978-1-4296-6069-3 (library binding)
  ISBN 978-1-4296-7109-5 (paperback)
  1. Magnets—Juvenile literature. 2. Magnetism—Juvenile literature. I. Title. II. Series.
  QC757.5.A47 2012
  538'.4—dc22   2010053932

Editorial Credits

Erika L. Shores, editor; Bobbie Nuytten and Ashlee Suker, designers; Wanda Winch, media researcher;
    Laura Manthe, production specialist

Photo Credits

All photos Capstone Studio/Karon Dubke except:
Shutterstock/Anton Balazh, 15, Levent Konuk, 19

Note to Parents and Teachers

The Science Builders series supports national science standards related to physical science.
This book describes and illustrates magnets. The images support early readers in understanding
the text. The repetition of words and phrases helps early readers learn new words. This book
also introduces early readers to subject-specific vocabulary words, which are defined in the
Glossary section. Early readers may need assistance to read some words and to use the Table of
Contents, Glossary, Read More, Internet Sites, and Index sections of the book.

Printed in the United States of America in Eau Claire, Wisconsin.
062013   007573R

Table of Contents

What Is a Magnet?

What makes a paper clip jump?
A magnet! Magnets are made
of iron, nickel, or steel.

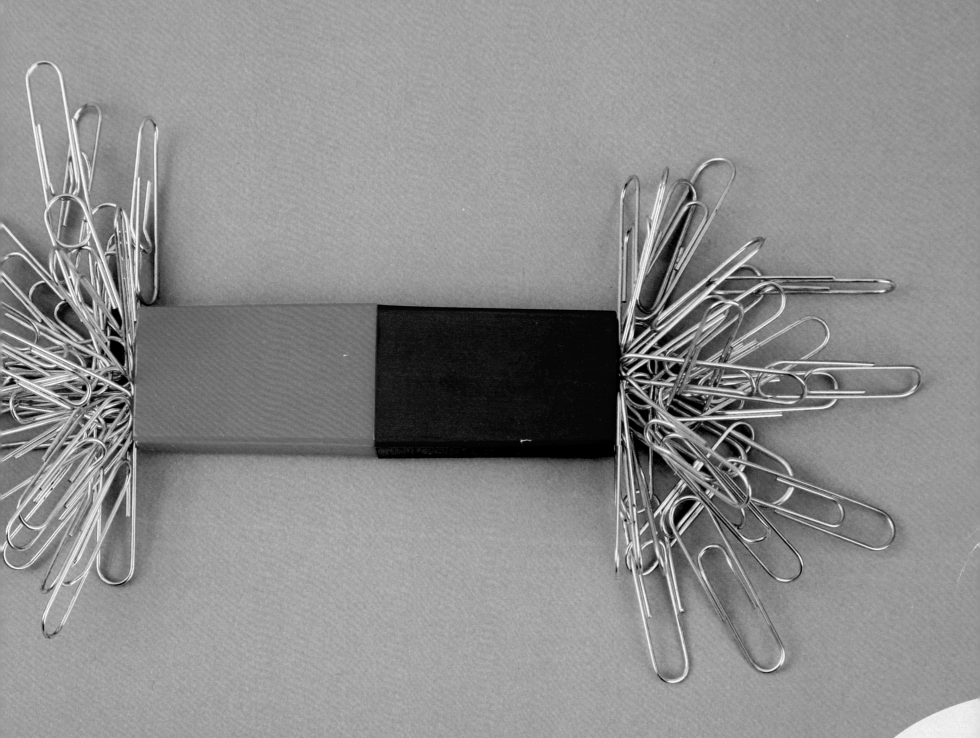

Magnets make some metal objects move. But magnets don't work on all metals. Can a magnet move an aluminum soda can? A copper penny?

How Magnets Work

An invisible area called
a magnetic field surrounds
a magnet. Iron filings show
the magnet's lines of energy.

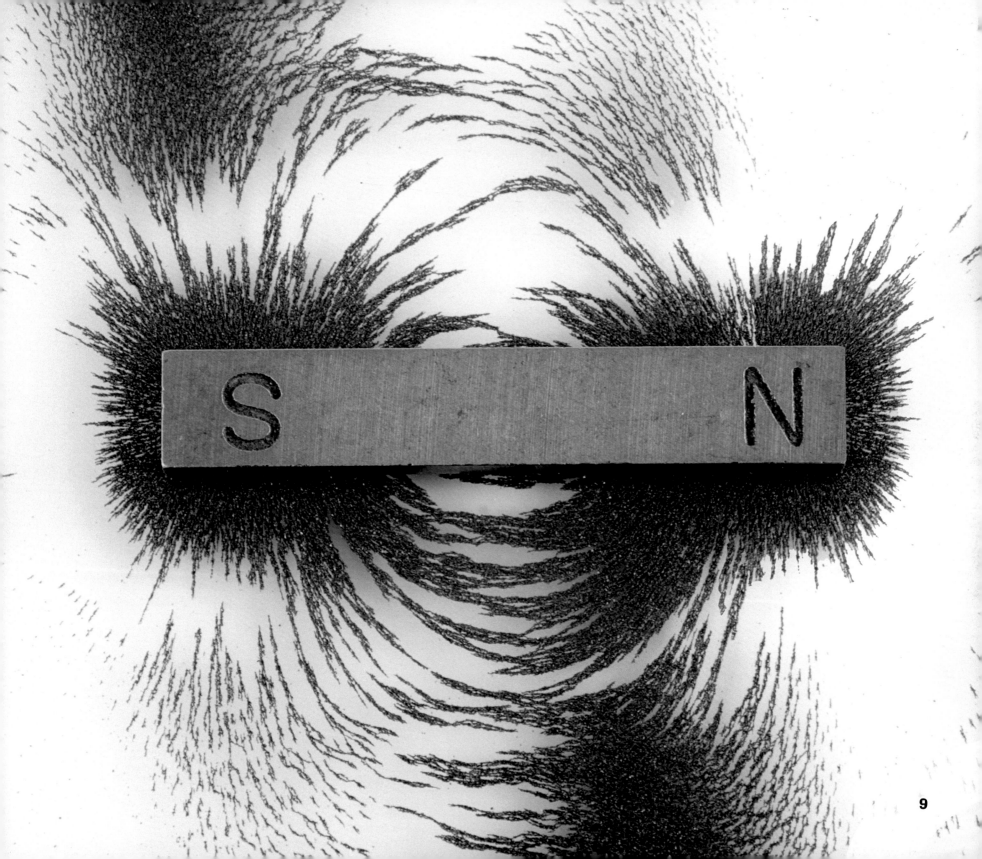

A magnet's pull is strongest at the spots with the most filings. These areas are called a magnet's poles. One end is north, and the other is south.

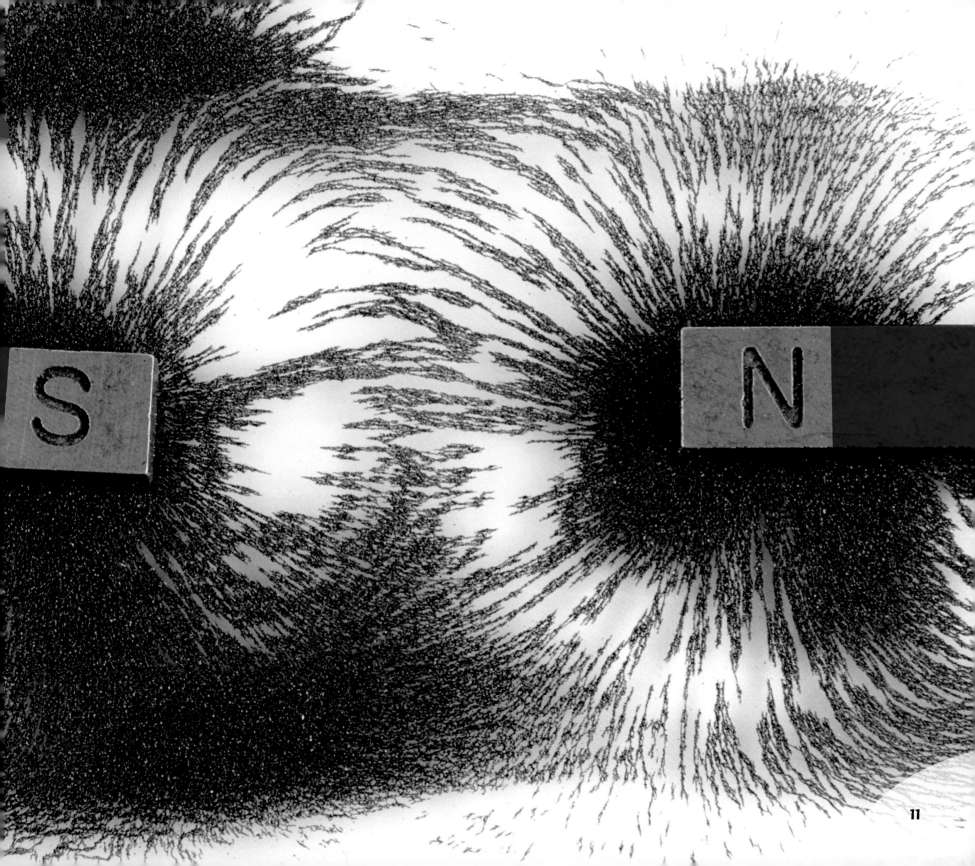

Try to make the north poles

of two magnets touch.

They will push away, or repel,

each other. But opposite poles

pull together, or attract.

Earth acts like a huge magnet.

It has a north pole

and a south pole.

North Pole

South Pole

Magnets at Work

Magnets show people where to go. A compass needle always points north. Earth's magnetic energy pulls it that way.

Magnets help doctors see
where you are hurt.
An MRI machine's powerful
magnet helps make a picture
of the inside of your body.

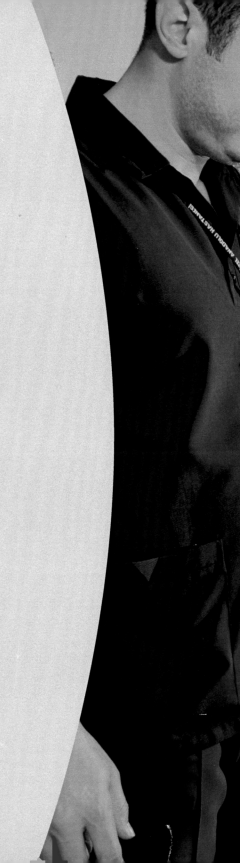